Written and Illustrated by Shoo Rayner

Dug's Bronze Age Family

Dug **Woof**

Over 3,000 years ago, Dug's family made

knives, axes and other things from bronze.

Join Dug as he braves a swarm of bees so

he can learn how to make a metal man.

Mini **Dad**

Chapter One

"I'm so bored!" sighed Dug.

"Help me make rock babies," said Mini.

"Rock babies?" Dug frowned. "What's that?"

Mini found a smooth pebble. She covered it in yellow grass to make hair, and tied it all around with a long piece of grass.

"You just scratch on some eyes and a mouth to make a face," she said. "And …"

"It's a rock baby!" Dug cheered. "Let's make more!"

Mini made beds out of leaves and sang lullabies to her rock babies.

"I'm going to make a rock man!" said Dug.

"Copy cat," said Mini. "It was my idea!"

Dug ignored her. He found a big, smooth stone and gave it lots of hair. He added a long stick for a hunting spear and a bent stick for an axe. Then he scratched a fierce-looking face on it.

"It looks just like Dad when he's hunting!"

Dug laughed. "It does not!" boomed Dad.

"I've got a beard ... and I've got legs too!"

The children laughed until their sides hurt. "And anyway," said Dad. "Today we're not hunting with spears. We are hunting with fire!"

Chapter Two

Dad pointed at a tree. A strange, moving

shape hung beneath a branch.

"Bees!" squeaked Mini.

"Bees mean honey!" Dug cheered.

"Mmmm!" the children licked their lips.

They used hot coals to make a fire.

They covered the fire with wet leaves
to make giant clouds of smoke.

"Smoke makes the bees go to sleep,"
said Dad. He tied a blade onto a stick.
"Dug, I want you to climb the tree and
cut down the honeycomb."

"Me!" Dug looked alarmed.

"I'm too big!" said Dad. "Make sure you
leave some honeycomb behind for the bees."

The bees hummed in a sleepy sort of way as Dug climbed the tree and reached out with his stick. The blade sliced through the honeycomb. A large chunk dropped into Dad's arms.

"Well done!" said Dad. "Now climb down carefully."

A bee landed on Dug's neck. "Ow!" Dug cried. "I've been stung!"

Dug wobbled and fell onto the soft leaves under the tree.

"I said climb down carefully!" Dad laughed.

"Ow! Ow! Ow!" yelled Dug. "It really, really hurts!"

Dad's hands were covered in honey. He rubbed some onto the sting. "That will soon make it better," he said.

Chapter Three

Dad heated a blade in the fire and sliced the wax off the top of the honeycomb. The beautiful, golden honey oozed and dripped into a bowl. Dug and Mini let the honey drip onto their fingers.

"Mmmmm!" they swooned as they licked the sweet, gooey liquid.

When every last drop of honey had dripped into the bowl, Dad took some honeycomb and squeezed it into a ball.

"This is beeswax," he explained. "You can use it for all sorts of things."

Dug watched Dad squeeze and squash the wax. As it warmed up in his hands, it became easier to make it into shapes. "Can I have some?" Dug asked. "I've got an idea."

Dad watched Dug pull the wax this way
and that.

"Look!" said Dug. "I've made a wax man!"

He held it up for them to see and admire.

"It looks just like me!" Dad laughed. "And
it's even got legs!"

Chapter Four

Dad made pots out of wet clay. He put his wax axe shapes and Dug's wax man inside them. Then he covered them with fine sand.

"When we pour hot, melted bronze into the hole at the top, the wax will melt and the bronze will fill the shape of the wax man," explained Dad. Dug was breathless with excitement.

Dad lit the fire and Dug pumped the bellows up and down.

"The bellows make more air," said Dad.

"More air makes the fire get very hot."

Soon the fire was roaring. Dad put the clay bowl in the fire. "We put copper and a little tinstone in this pot and wait for it to melt," he said.

Soon a liquid, golden yellow metal shimmered in the pot.

Dug helped Dad lift the pot out of the fire with long, wet sticks. Carefully they poured the liquid metal into the axe moulds.

"There's just enough left," said Dad, as they poured the last of the molten bronze into Dug's metal man mould.

"Now we wait for it to cool down," said Dad.

Chapter Five

Dug jumped up and down with excitement.

"Can we look now?" he asked.

"Has it cooled down yet?"

Dad flicked the axe heads out of their stone moulds and examined them.

"They're cool enough to handle," he smiled.

"Go on, then. Open up your mould."

"Wahay!" Dug pulled his mould to pieces.
The sand fell away revealing a burnt,
muddy shape inside.

"It needs a wash" said Dad.

In no time, the mud washed off revealing
a wonderful, bright, shiny metal man
underneath.

Dug held it up so they could all see it.

"This is Metal Man!" he said, in a metal
man voice.

Wow!" said Dad. "He's amazing! He looks just like me!" Mini's eyes opened wide as she stared at the metal man. Then a big smile spread across her face.

"We could make metal babies!" she suggested.

Dug looked at her and sighed.

"Copy cat!" he said.

Bronze Age Facts

In the Bronze Age, melting metals became common. Bronze (a mixture of tin and copper) was melted and poured into clay moulds. When the metal cooled, it formed into the shape of the mould. Nature provided useful tools, too. Most medicines were made from plants. Honey is a good remedy for bee stings, as Dad discovered when he used it on Dug's stings.

Franklin Watts
First published in Great Britain in 2016
by The Watts Publishing Group

Text and Illustrations © Shoo Rayner 2016

Series Editor: Melanie Palmer
Series Advisor: Catherine Glavina
Series Designers: Peter Scoulding
and Cathryn Gilbert

ISBN 978 1 4451 4806 9 (hbk)
ISBN 978 1 4451 4808 3 (pbk)
ISBN 978 1 4451 4807 6 (library ebook)

Printed in China

FSC
www.fsc.org

MIX
Paper from
responsible sources
FSC® C104740

Franklin Watts
An imprint of
Hachette Children's Group
Part of The Watts Publishing Group
Carmelite House
50 Victoria Embankment
London EC4Y 0DZ

An Hachette UK Company
www.hachette.co.uk

www.franklinwatts.co.uk